Gaddafi and Other Selections on American Foreign Policy

Restoring the African Mind Research Collection

CONTENTS

1 GADDAFI AND WESTERN IMPERIALISM

In the speech that President Woodrow Wilson gave before Congress in an attempt to get them to declare war against Germany, Wilson explained:

> The world must be made safe for democracy. Its peace must be planted upon the tested foundations of political liberty. We have no selfish ends to serve. We desire no conquest, no dominion. We seek no indemnities for ourselves, no material compensation for the sacrifices we shall freely make. We are but one of the champions of the rights of mankind. We shall be satisfied when those rights have been made as secure as the faith and the freedom of nations can make them.

The reality here was that Wilson had failed to make America safe for democracy, especially where African people are concerned. Wilson was a staunch segregationist. Yet this man, who could not achieve racial equality and equal rights in America, felt that it was America's mission to secure the rights of mankind.

In this speech Wilson began a pattern of America acting as a sort of global police force, intervening in or invading countries under the guise of spreading democracy. This is in reality a continuation of the Western legacy of trying to spread civilization and Christianity throughout the world through conquest. Of course, democracy, civilization, and Christianity are all disguises for the West's true intentions when they do invade other countries. Moreover, rarely, if ever, has American intervention achieved the goal of spreading democracy. Rather than making the world safer for democracy, such American intervention has often led to destabilization and to the exacerbation of the problem that intervention was meant to solve. It is within this historical tradition that I would locate the American intervention in Libya.

President Barack Obama has admitted that his worst mistake as president was "failing to plan for the day after, what I think was the right thing to do, in intervening in Libya." President Obama initially celebrated the overthrow of Gaddafi. In a speech to the United Nations General Assembly, Obama declared:

> One year ago, the people of Libya were ruled by the world's longest-serving dictator. But faced with bullets and bombs and a dictator who threatened to hunt them down like rats, they showed relentless bravery. We will never forget the words of the Libyan who stood up in those early days of the revolution and said, "Our words are free now." It's a feeling you can't explain. Day after day, in the face of

bullets and bombs, the Libyan people refused to give back that freedom. And when they were threatened by the kind of mass atrocity that often went unchallenged in the last century, the United Nations lived up to its charter. The Security Council authorized all necessary measures to prevent a massacre. The Arab League called for this effort; Arab nations joined a NATO-led coalition that halted Qaddafi's forces in their tracks.

In the months that followed, the will of the coalition proved unbreakable, and the will of the Libyan people could not be denied. Forty-two years of tyranny was ended in six months. From Tripoli to Misurata to Benghazi—today, Libya is free. Yesterday, the leaders of a new Libya took their rightful place beside us, and this week, the United States is reopening our embassy in Tripoli.

In the years that followed things would decline very quickly in Libya. This would include extremists in Libya killing the American ambassador J. Christopher Stevens in 2012. As the situation continued to deteriorate in Libya, Obama was eventually forced to recognize the reality that the American involvement in Libya was a failure. America had once again helped to destabilize a nation through supporting forced regime change. Given America's history the results are hardly surprising.

In an interview with Chris Wallace, a news anchor from Fox News, Obama was asked about what he considered to be his greatest failure as president. Obama admitted that his failure to prepare for the aftermath of Gaddafi being deposed in Libya was what he considered to be his greatest mistake. Obama also explained that he felt it was "the right thing to do." The problem is that American intervention is always framed as being "the right thing to do." During the Cold War deposing democratically elected leaders to defend against the spread of communism was considered the "right thing to do." In intervening in other countries to do the right thing, America frequently ends up doing the wrong thing because of its failure to prepare for the aftermath of its interventions.

As is the general pattern with such cases of American intervention, Muammar Gaddafi was an American ally shortly before the intervention. This was not always the case. American discomfort with the Gaddafi regime began from the onset. Gaddafi came to power in 1969 following the overthrow of King Idris. His relationship with Western countries was strained since then. The lowest point came during the 1980s when Ronald Reagan ordered Tripoli to be bombed in an attempt to assassinate Gaddafi. Libya was also accused of being involved in several terrorist attacks, including one in Berlin that killed two Americans. The United States saw Gaddafi as a terrorist threat that needed to be eliminated.

In the later years of his regime, Gaddafi's relationship with the West became much closer. The relationship between Gaddafi and the West was such that Britain's MI6 assisted Gaddafi by capturing Abdel Hakim Belhaj, who was then taken to Libya where he was abused by Gaddafi's regime. Belhaj reported that he was initially captured and detained by the American CIA, who tortured him before sending him to Libya. It was the MI6 that provided information about Belhaj's whereabouts to the CIA. Gaddafi became so close with the West that Britain and the United States were assisting Gaddafi with capturing and torturing critics of Gaddafi's regime. MI6 operated in Libya until the revolution against Gaddafi started.

One of the aspects of Gaddafi's regime that went ignored during the intervention was that Gaddafi had provided real benefits to the Libyan people. A country study of Libya that was done in 1987, at a time when Gaddafi was considered to be a supporter of terrorism by the West, stated of his regime:

> Subsidized food, inexpensive housing, free medical care and education, and profit-sharing were among the benefits that eased the lives of all citizens. The government protected the employed in their jobs and subsidized the underemployed and unemployed. In addition, there were nurseries to care for the children of working mothers, orphanages for homeless children, and homes for the aged. The welfare programs had reached even the oasis towns of the desert, where they reportedly were received with considerable satisfaction. The giving of alms to the poor remained one of the pillars of the Islamic faith, but the extent of public welfare was such that there was increasingly less place for private welfare.

The study also notes:

> The streets of Tripoli and Benghazi were kept scrupulously clean, and drinking water in these cities was of good quality. The government had

made significant efforts to provide safe water. In summing up accomplishments since 1970, officials listed almost 1,500 wells drilled and more than 900 reservoirs in service in 1985, in addition to 9,000 kilometers of potable water networks and 44 desalination plants. Sewage disposal had also received considerable attention, twenty-eight treatment plants having been built.

Of education the report states:

> In 1987 education was free at all levels, and university students received substantial stipends. Attendance was compulsory between the ages of six and fifteen years or until completion of the preparatory cycle of secondary school.

Gaddafi was not the typical strongman ruler that had exploited his nation's resources solely for the benefit of himself, while giving nothing back to his people. Even so, Gaddafi's government was not immune to criticisms from segments of the population that were dissatisfied with his rule. Gaddafi's relationship with university students was especially interesting in this regard. Gaddafi had made education on all levels free, including university education. Under King Idris the first university in Libya had opened in 1955 and under Gaddafi enrollment increased significantly. In encouraging education Gaddafi was also helping to breed dissent in Libya, as university students became some of the most vocal critics of his government's policies. In 1976, students violently protested in

Benghazi and Tripoli over compulsory military training. Ten years later, in 1986, students resisted Gaddafi's attempts to close their departments and destroy their libraries as part of his campaign to Arabize the nation and eliminate Western influences.

Much of this conflict was centered on the government's attempts to establish control over student unions for the purposes of the Arab Socialist Union (ASU) political party, as the country study points out:

> A particularly serious incident occurred in January 1976 when students at the University of Benghazi protested government interference in student union elections. Elected students who were not ASU members were considered officially unacceptable by the authorities. Security forces moved onto the campus, and violence resulted. Reports that several students were shot and killed in the incident were adamantly denied by the government. Nonetheless, sympathizers organized more protests.

As we have seen, despite the repressive and dictatorial structure of the regime, Libya was stable and the Libyan masses were not living in a state of massive neglect and poverty as had been seen in so many other African nations. In celebrating the overthrow of Gaddafi, Western leaders failed to acknowledge the stability of Libya under Gaddafi, which would later prove to be a marked contrast to the state of affairs in the years following Gaddafi's overthrow.

Gaddafi was someone who was greatly influenced by Gamal Nasser's vision of Pan-Arabism and anti-imperialism. The problem for Gaddafi is that, much like Nasser, he found little success with his efforts to unite Arabs. Nasser's successor was Anwar Sadat, who did not share Nasser's commitment to Pan-Arabism. The differences between Sadat and Gaddafi resulted in a brief border conflict between the two nations in 1977. As Obama mentioned in the speech that was quoted previously, the Arab League itself called for intervention in Libya to protect the protestors.

Whereas Gaddafi was attempting to unite Arabs, he was somewhat of a destabilizing force among Africans given how often he intervened in African conflicts. In 1978, Uganda launched an invasion into Tanzania. The resulting war between Uganda and Tanzania led to Idi Amin being ousted from Uganda. Gaddafi decided to support Amin's failed assault on Tanzania by providing supplies and even soldiers. Gaddafi also intervened in the conflict between Eritrea and Ethiopia. Gaddafi initially supported Eritrea against the government of Haile Selassie, before switching his support to Ethiopia following the coup in Ethiopia. Senegal and Gambia also broke diplomatic relations with Libya, claiming that Gaddafi had been supporting dissident groups in those countries.

There was also the matter of Gaddafi's territorial war with Chad, which resulted in an eventual victory for Chad. In the 1970s, Libya decided to invade Chad and annex the Aouzou Strip. So sure was Libya of their claims over the territory that starting in the mid-1970s, Libyan maps included the Aouzou Strip as being in Libya. Much of this conflict took place in the backdrop of Chad's civil war, which Libya intervened in to support the rebel forces in their attempt to overthrow the government of Chad. Libya's involvement in the

Chadian war only made matters worse.

In 1979, Goukouni Oueddei was installed as president in Chad, with the support of Libya. By 1983, Goukouni was overthrown by Hissène Habré. Oueddei went into exile in Libya where he reorganized his forces and fought to regain control of Chad. As the fighting continued in Chad, Libya continued its support of anti-government forces. It was also with Libyan support that Idriss Déby was able to overthrow Habré in 1990. In effect, Libya had contributed greatly to the instability in Chad from the 1970s until 1990.

It should not be overlooked that Gaddafi did provide support for the African National Congress at a time when America and Britain considered the ANC to be a terrorist organization, and for this Nelson Mandela was always grateful. When questioned by Ken Adelman about his continued support of Gaddafi, despite Gaddafi's poor human rights record, Mandela responded by saying: "One of the mistakes which some political analysts make is to think their enemies should be our enemies." This response was met with applause and it was also a very profound statement regarding American foreign policy because Mandela was himself branded as a terrorist by some American politicians. America's definition of an "enemy" is typically based on whether or not that individual is useful for helping to advance America's interests. When America was aligned with the racist regime in South Africa, Mandela was labeled as a terrorist for opposing that regime. This was the case with Gaddafi as well. Gaddafi ceased being an American enemy so long as he served America's interests, but when the protests against him started he was quickly abandoned by his newfound Western allies. The same countries that helped him torture dissidents were now actively helping the rebels to overthrow him. As Obama admitted, however, no consideration was made for what would happen when Gaddafi was gone.

In expressing the views that he did, Mandela was expressing a fairly consistent and reasonable foreign policy in which South Africa remained supportive of those who supported South Africa's struggle. Mandela did not seek to defend the abuses of Gaddafi's regime—although he did not acknowledge them in his response to Adelman either—but he also refused to abandon a man that had supported his struggle. Western foreign policy typically does not operate out of this same commitment to loyalty and appreciation, which is why Western countries were so quick to turn against Gaddafi after helping him to capture dissidents in the past.

Western intervention in Libya helped to destabilize the nation by overthrowing the government there, but this was the same thing that Gaddafi had done to Chad and had attempted to do in Tanzania, so in a sense Gaddafi's overthrow was a case of the chickens coming home to roost, as Malcolm X would put it. Gaddafi's foreign policy was marked by his support of rebel groups in other countries. When Gaddafi faced an uprising from rebel groups within his own country, the international community moved to intervene in Libya on behalf of the rebel groups which were protesting for an end to Gaddafi's regime.

The protests against Gaddafi turned into a civil war between Gaddafi's supporters and the rebels. The North Atlantic Treaty Organization (NATO) decided to involve itself in conflict in Libya by imposing a no fly zone over Libya and assisted the rebels in Libya through airstrikes. Eventually the rebels were able to successfully overthrow Gaddafi and kill him. Little concern was given to what may happen in Libya with Gaddafi gone or what would happen to the many positive policies that Gaddafi implemented in Libya.

The consequence of the instability in Libya would result in four State Department employees who were stationed in Libya being killed, including Ambassador J. Christopher Stevens. In the remarks which Obama delivered to honor Stevens and others who were killed, Obama stated that "we hold our head high, knowing that because of these patriots, because of you, this country that we love will always shine as a light unto the world." These were nice sentiments which expressed a very idealistic view of America, but Obama's sentiments were simply at odds with the reality of America's policies in the rest of the world. I would argue that the sentiments expressed by Obama are part of the problem.

American leaders like Obama seem to view America as a shining light for the rest of the world and this sense of self-righteousness leads to actions such as the intervention in Libya. Obama explained that he felt intervening in Libya was the right thing to do, but he also admitted that the worst failure of his presidency was failing to plan for the aftermath of the intervention. Why would one intervene in a nation for the purpose of helping to topple a leader who had been in power for decades without preparing for the possibility that doing so could lead to instability? This failure to plan is especially astonishing when one considers that the safety of American citizens such as Stevens depended on Libya being stable. A destabilized Libya is not only a threat to the people of Libya, but to the Americans who are in Libya.

The disastrous American intervention in Libya may have been by Obama's own admission, the worst mistake of his presidency, but it is more than that. It represented the continuing legacy of failed American interventions, which only create more problems than they solve. Yet, as I noted before, for Gaddafi it was a case of chickens coming home to roost.

Selected References:

Helen Chapin Metz, ed. *Libya: A Country Study*. Washington: GPO for the Library of Congress, 1987.

Martin Chulov, "MI6 knew I was tortured, says Libyan rebel leader," *The Guardian*, September 5, 2011.

Martin Meredith, *The Fate of Africa*

Peter Baker, David D. Kirkpatrick, and Suliman Ali Zway, "Diplomats' Bodies Return to U.S., and Libyan Guards Recount Deadly Riot," *New York Times*, September 14, 2012.

Remarks by President Obama in Address to the United Nations General Assembly, September 21, 2011.

Woodrow Wilson, "Safe for Democracy," April 2, 1917.

2 THE CONSEQUENCES OF BLOWBACK

The support which Christopher Hitchens provided for the Iraq War was somewhat surprising to some who had viewed Hitchens as someone who had been very critical of imperialism. Interestingly, Hitchens attempted to frame his support for the Iraq War as support for an anti-imperial war. Hitchens argued that everything that the United States did in Iraq since 1968 was imperial. He noted that the United States helped to install the Baath party of Saddam Hussein, that the United States had promised support to the Kurds only to sell the Kurds out, and that Hussein was given a greenlight by Jimmy Carter to invade Iran. Hitchens explained that the war between Iraq and Iran resulted in at least one million and a half casualties. Given this history, Hitchens argued that it would have been an act of imperialism not to intervene and to leave Iraq as it is. Hitchens explained that the intervention in 2003 was the first time that he was aware of in which the United States intervened in Iraq on the right side and Hitchens explained that he was proud to have supported such an intervention. Hitchens' argument was that the United

States had consistently done the wrong thing in Iraq since the 1960s and that the intervention to overthrow Hussein was the right thing to do.

From 1958 to 1960, Dwight Eisenhower's administration had aided Kassem against Iran. By 1961, Kassem had grown more assertive. This included seeking arms, quarreling with Kuwait, and threatening Western oil interests. Kassem came to be viewed as a regional threat that needed to be removed. In 1963, Britain and Israel supported an American intervention in Iraq. Kassem stepped down following a coup. He was executed and replaced by the Baath Party. Saddam was a member of this party. Saddam had previously been forced to flee from Iraq after he was involved in a failed assassination attempt against Kassem in 1958, with Kassem out of power, the Baathists began to systematically eliminate Iraq's educated elite. Hundreds of doctors, teachers, technicians, and lawyers were murdered. This did not seem to concern the United States, which sent arms to the new regime in Iraq. The United States would later find itself invading Iraq and toppling Saddam, the very dictator that America had supported in the past.

It is true that Saddam Hussein was a brutal dictator who was helped into power by the United States. Even if removing him from power was the morally correct thing for the United States to do, the invasion itself was managed very poorly. In the first place, the invasion of Iraq was not presented as merely being a mission to topple a brutal dictator. The invasion of Iraq was justified under the pretense that Saddam Hussein had weapons of mass destruction.

It turned out that there were no weapons of mass destruction. Colin Powell, who delivered a speech before the United Nations in 2003 in which he made the case for the American intervention in Iraq, later expressed regret over giving the speech. Powell explained that he spent four days at the CIA to make sure all of the intelligence was correct. He was given assurances that the information was correct, but it turned out that the information was wrong.

That the invasion was justified by inaccurate information did not seem to bother Bush. In fact, Bush publicly joked about the missing weapons of mass destruction, even displaying photos of himself looking for the weapons of mass destruction in the Oval Office. The joke was met with applause and laughter from the audience. Thomas Young, a veteran of the Iraq War, did not appreciate the joke. He described the joke as being callous. It indeed was callous for Bush to make light of the fact that American soldiers were sent to fight and die over a claim which turned out to be false.

Yet another problem with the invasion of Iraq was that the United States and its partners did not have a real plan for what to do after removing Saddam Hussein from power. This was the view expressed by Iraqi satirist Ahmed Albasheer. Albasheer explained that the invading countries' policies towards Iraq were a disaster. Government positions were allocated based on identity rather than merit. The Iraqi army was disbanded, which left hundreds of thousands of men in poverty. Moreover, people with no government experience were put in charge. During this time, Albasheer experienced a number of tragedies. A mortar fell on his house, killing his brother. He explained that the family had to scrape his brother's remains from the wall in order to have something to bury. Albasheer's father was tortured by Al-Qaeda and died a year later.

Albasheer's cousin was also killed after stepping on an IED.

Whereas Hitchens felt a sense of pride over the American decision to overthrow Saddam Hussein, Albasheer, who had to live with the consequences of this intervention, concluded that the attempt to save Iraq in 2003 did not go so well. That the intervention did not go so well was a product of the fact that the intervention was poorly planned. Following the 9/11 terrorist attacks, President Bush wondered if Saddam Hussein had been involved. No link between Iraq and the attack had been uncovered. In reality, Osama bin Laden resented Saddam Hussein's regime. Even so, it seemed that the United States was eager to see the removal of Saddam Hussein and the claim about weapons of mass destruction provided a pretense to support the invasion. Hitchens, who was also eager to see the fall of Hussein's dictatorship, supported this invasion. One may grant that Hitchens' reason for supporting the invasion was correct. Saddam Hussein was a brutal dictator who needed to be removed, but the invasion was carried out by an administration which was relying on false information and appeared indifferent to the devastating consequences of the war. Hitchens correctly noted that America had consistently gotten it wrong with Iraq. The invasion of Iraq demonstrated that even when America did do the right thing in Iraq, it was done for the wrong reason and carried out in the wrong manner. Hitchens attempted to suggest that his support for the Iraq War was an anti-imperial position, but he was ultimately simply attempting to defend and rationalize yet another failure on the part of the American empire.

The problems with the intervention in Iraq also

demonstrate the larger problem of American policy in the Middle East.

In an interview with Fox News, Hillary Clinton noted that the United States contributed to the problem in Afghanistan. The United States armed the mujahadeen forces against the Soviet Union in Afghanistan. This effort was successful, as the Soviet Union was driven out of Afghanistan, but years later the United States would return to Afghanistan to fight some of the very people which they had supported against the Soviet Union.

The CIA created the term "blowback," which refers to the unintended consequences of American foreign policy and intervention. This not only happened in Libya, Iraq, and Afghanistan, but also in Iran as well. President Eisenhower approved of a coup against Prime Minister Mohammad Mossadegh. Mossadegh's goal was to modernize and democratize Iran, which put him at odds with the nation's monarch, Mohammad Reza (the Shah). Mossadegh also wanted to nationalize Iran's oil fields. This outraged BP and the British government so much so that they determined that Mossadegh had to be removed. Together the United States and Britain plotted the overthrow of Mossadegh. The plot involved bribing journalists, editors, Islamic preachers, and others to enhance public hostility and distrust of Mossadegh. Thugs were also hired to carry out staged attacks against religious leaders to make it appear as though Mossadegh had ordered these attacks. On the day of the coup, thousands of paid demonstrators converged on parliament to demand that Mossadegh be dismissed. The plan was a success.

With Mossadegh removed, the Shah was returned to the throne. Shah Reza was a pro-American leader who established a repressive regime. This included the creation of the Savak, which were a secret police force which were known for their brutality. These abuses did not concern America, which was very eager to arm the government of Iran. Iran became America's single largest arms purchaser.

In 1979, Iran experienced a revolution. Protesters took to the street to cry "Death to the American Shah." These uprisings were led by an Islamic cleric named Ayatollah Ruhollah Khomeini. Unlike the pro-American shah, Khomeini held a very hostile view towards the West. The 1979 revolution overthrew a pro-American dictatorship and replaced it with a regime which was hostile towards America. This hostility was displayed when students in Iran broke into the American embassy and took 52 Americans as hostages. It would take 444 days before the hostages were released.

It was mentioned before that the United States supported Saddam Hussein. In 1980, Hussein decided to invade Iran. The United States intervened in this war by providing intelligence to Iraq, as well as arms. During the war, Hussein used chemical weapons against Iranians. The United States was aware of this, but supported Hussein in the war, nevertheless.

The United States was making deals with Iran as well. Iran made a secret request to buy weapons from the United States. The United States entered talks with Iran and struck a deal. Iran would help with the release of American hostages who were being held in Lebanon in return for the weapons. America overcharged the Iranians for the weapons and used the surplus to fund the Contras who were trying to overthrow the government of Nicaragua.

3 AMERICAN FOREIGN POLICY AND "THAT RELIGION"

One of the problems with America's foreign policy in the Arab world has been a lack of willingness to accept that the United States has been complicit in much of the violence and unrest in the Arab world. This topic came up on Bill Maher's program. Glenn Greenwald and he spoke about America's support for Mubarak's dictatorship in Egypt. Greenwald also noted that Maher is a citizen of America, a country which has generated more violence in the world over the last six decades than Arab countries have done.

Maher offered some very weak responses, such as disingenuously suggesting that Greenwald was trying to claim that all of the problems in the Arab world are America's fault. Greenwald responded that it is not all America's fault, but that America should take responsibility for its actions. Maher then responded, "That religion goes back a thousand years before our revolution, so I don't think we can take all the blame."

The one line exposed the problem with Maher's thinking about the Arab world. In his view the problem in those countries is "that religion." I certainly agree that religion should be criticized to the extent that extremists use religion to impose oppressive theocratic governments on people, but the point which Greenwald was making is that the United States should take accountability for supporting dictatorships and overthrowing governments in the Arab world.

Another example of this issue came up when Ron Paul mentioned that the United States was attacked during 9/11 because America had bases in Saudi Arabia. Paul was booed by members of the audience, but what he was trying to get them to understand was that Arab hostility towards Americans was rooted in American aggression in the region. Ron Paul also mentioned that America has been bombing and killing hundreds of thousands of Iraqis.

One thing which I found to be admirable about Ron Paul was his honesty about the impact of American foreign policy in the Arab world. On another occasion, Paul spoke about "blowback" from American intervention. He noted that Hamas was encouraged by Israel to counteract Yasser Arafat of the Palestinian Liberation Organization. He pointed out that the United States then encouraged elections in Palestine. The result was that Hamas was elected.

American intervention often caused more problems than it has resolved. It is very easy for commentators such as Bill Maher to blame the problem on the Islamic religion, but Greenwald was correct to note that America does share some of the blame for the problems in those countries as well. Blaming Islam is a way to minimize the American role in this problem.

4 9/11 AND OSAMA BIN LADEN'S LEGACY OF TERROR

In western Asia, Islam emerged as a very powerful force. The religion was spread by the Prophet Muhammad who began preaching about the one true god, Allah. The Prophet Muhammad claimed that the revelations which he preached were communicated to him by an angel. At this time the people of Arabia practiced a pagan religion. Muhammad's teachings were not well-received, but he was eventually able to establish power over the city of Mecca and established Islam as the most dominant religion in Arabia.

Following the death of Muhammad, Islam spread very rapidly due to Islamic conquests. Syria, Damascus, Palmyra, Antioch, and Jerusalem all fell under Arab domination. In 637, the Arab Muslim forces defeated Persia. These conquests spread into North Africa as well. Arabs conquered Egypt. The conquest continued into Tunisia and Algeria. Queen Kahina is remembered for her valiant defense in the face of the Arab invasion in North Africa, but she was ultimately defeated and killed.

According to the North African historian Ibn Khaldun, Islam served a unifying force for Arabs. He explained: "Arab pride, touchiness and intense jealousy of power render it impossible for them to agree. Only when their nature has been permeated by a religious impulse are they transformed, so that the tendency to anarchy is replaced by a spirit of mutual defense. Consider the moment when religion dominated their policy and led them to observe a religious law designed to promote the moral and material interests of civilization. Under a series of successors to the Prophet [Muhammad], how vast their empire became and how strongly was it established."

The spread of Islam was not merely the spread of a religion. It also spread Arabic culture and the Arabic language throughout the region. Islam helped to produce a distinct regional Arab identity which came to include people who were not ethnically Arab but had adopted Arabic culture and the religion of Islam.

From 1514 to 1638, the Ottoman state of the Turks managed to conquer nearly all the Arab countries. The Ottoman Empire would eventually fall during World War I. The collapse of the Ottoman Empire would have profound consequences for the region. Arab states which had been under Ottoman rule for centuries found themselves under the hegemony of European colonial powers. Vladimir Borisovich Lutsky gave the following description of the situation: "Though free at last from the Turkish yoke, they had been cheated of their long-awaited independence and fallen under the influence of the British and French colonialists. The end of World War I opened a new period in the history of the Arab people, a period of struggle against British and French imperialism for the complete national liberation of the Arab countries."

After Arab countries freed themselves from the domination of British and French imperialism, they were then confronted with the regional influence of the United States, which had frequently intervened in the region to overthrow certain governments or to support regimes which served American interests, even if those regimes were oppressive. I recount this history because the terrorism of Osama bin Laden and other Islamic extremist groups developed in part as a response to Western hegemony over the Islamic world. Bin Laden himself invoked the history of the clash between the Christian Westernized civilization and the Islamic Arabic civilization by referring to Americans as "Crusaders", which is a reference to the Crusade in Europe, which was an attempt to save the Holy Land from Muslim rule.

Osama bin Laden was born in Saudi Arabia. He was the seventeenth of his father's fifty-seven children. In 1979, the Soviet Union intervened in Afghanistan in support of the communist government which was established there in 1978. Muslims from around the world flocked to Afghanistan to join this "holy war" against the Soviet Union. Bin Laden was among those who went to Afghanistan to fight the Soviets. The Afghan forces finally defeated the Soviet Union in 1988. Bin Laden's role in this conflict helped to increase his stature in the Islamic world. This would later help him to organize his campaign of terror against the United States.

In 1990, Saddam Hussein invaded Kuwait. Bin Laden proposed to the Saudi monarchy that mujahadeen be used to retake Kuwait. Saudi Arabia instead decided to seek the military assistance of the

United States. The Saudi royal family also allowed American forces to establish a base in Saudi Arabia. This outraged bin Laden who despised the idea that American soldiers were allowed to be stationed in Saudi Arabia. Bin Laden left the country and in 1994 his citizenship was revoked.

Bin Laden moved to Sudan in 1991. There bin Laden used his construction company to build a new highway in Sudan. Bin Laden had established connections to the government of Sudan in 1989 when Hassan al Turabi requested bin Laden's assistance with fighting the war against African Christians in the south. While in Sudan, bin Laden also supported anti-Saddam Islamists in Iraq. Turabi reportedly got bin Laden to agree to cease supporting anti-Saddam groups in Iraq. Bin Laden's tendency to support radical Islamic organizations in the region would create problems for him in Sudan.

The government of Sudan was receiving pressure from the United States and other nations to cease harboring terrorist organizations. Libya was also one of those nations which pressured Sudan. The Libyans who were members of bin Laden's army were forced to leave Sudan. In secret meetings with Saudi officials, Sudan offered to expel bin Laden to Saudi Arabia. Saudi officials wanted bin Laden out of Sudan, but they were also not willing to allow him to return to Saudi Arabia. Bin Laden no longer felt safe in Sudan, so he decided to leave in 1996. He returned to Afghanistan, which at this point was under Taliban rule. It was in Afghanistan that bin Laden launched his jihad against the United States.

In Afghanistan, bin Laden was given the freedom to publish his appeals for jihad. Unlike in Sudan, the government of Afghanistan allowed Al Qaeda members to freely travel throughout the country. Al Qaeda also used state-owned planes to bring money into the country. Around this time, bin Laden was also apparently working towards cooperation with Saddam Hussein. Hussein was trying to rebuild relations with the Saudis, however. This led him to avoid bin Laden.

Bin Laden was outraged over the presence of American soldiers in Saudi Arabia. He also denounced the American support of Israel and the suffering of the Iraqi people because of the sanctions which were imposed on them after the Gulf War. Bin Laden's solution was to declare a war against "Jews and Crusaders" to liberate the holy places from these intruders. He made it very apparent that in this war against the United States not even American civilians would be safe. When asked if he approved of attacks on civilians, bin Laden stated: "We do not have to differentiate between military or civilian. As far as we are concerned, they are all targets."

Bin Laden's campaign of terror included bombing the American embassies in Tanzania and Kenya in 1998. The attack in Kenya killed 12 Americans and 201 others, most of whom were Kenyans. Another 5,000 were injured. The attack on the embassy in Tanzania killed 11 people, none of which were Americans. Al Qaeda was also responsible for bombing the USS Cole in 2000. The attack killed 17 members of the ship's crew and wounded 40 others. Bin Laden's most notorious attack would come in 2001.

Prior to the attack on September 11, 2001, there were reports of a possible terrorist attack involving hijacked planes. The 9/11 Commission Report noted that in 1998 there were reports of a possible Al Qaeda plan to hijack a plane. There was also mention of a possible plot to fly an explosive-laden aircraft into an American city. In August of that same year, the intelligence community received information that a group of Libyans were hoping to crash a plane into the World Trade Center. None of this information could be corroborated, however. In August 1999, the Federal Aviation Administration's Civil Aviation Security intelligence office concluded that a suicide hijacking operation was unlikely because it would not offer an opportunity for dialogue to achieve the goal of obtaining Omar Abdel Rahman and other captives. It concluded that suicide hijacking was an option of "last resort." At the time Rahman was serving a life sentence for his role in the 1993 plot to blow up sites in New York City.

The 9/11 Commission Report indicated that officials were aware of the possibility of a terrorist attack involving hijacked planes. The 9/11 Commission Report also indicated that this possibility was not treated as a top national security priority. Prior to 9/11, Al Qaeda itself had not been treated as a top national security priority. In 2000 and during the first eight months of 2001, terrorism was not a major public concern. That would change after the events on September 11, 2001.

On the morning of September 11, four planes were hijacked. Most of what is known about the hijacking came from Betty Ong and Madeline "Amy" Sweeney, who were two flight attendants that were onboard one of the hijacked planes. The hijackers had stabbed two unarmed flight attendants and forced their way into the cockpit. How they were able to enter the cockpit is not known, but once inside the cockpit the hijackers sprayed an irritant to force the passengers to the rear of the plane. Contact with Sweeney and Ong was lost minutes before the plane crashed into the first tower.

The North Tower was the first of the two towers to be hit. Hundreds of civilians were killed by the impact of the plane smashing into the building. Hundreds more were trapped. Some of those who were trapped inside the building decided to jump out. The impact from the plane made all three of the building's stairwells impassable from the 92nd floor up. The impact also sent a fireball down the building, which blew out the elevators and burned civilians who were caught in the path of the fireball.

Seventeen minutes after the first tower was hit, the South Tower was struck by another plane. Unlike in the North Tower, the plane which hit the South Tower did leave portions of the building undamaged on the impact floors. One of the stairwells remained passable from the 91st floor down. The destruction caused by the two plane crashes resulted in both towers eventually collapsing. The South Tower was the first to collapse, followed by the North Tower. More than 2,900 Americans were killed because of this attack.

The third plane to crash was American Airlines Flight 77. This one struck the Pentagon, killing all the passengers on board as well as many civilians and military personnel who were in the building. United Airlines Flight 93 was the last of the four planes to leave the airport. The passengers on this flight received calls from family, friends, and colleagues about the two planes which hit the World Trade Center. Two of the callers from the flight reported that the hijackers were aware that the passengers were making calls but, the hijackers did not seem to care. The callers also reported that a passenger had been stabbed and two people were lying on the floor in the cabin, injured or dead. Several callers indicated that the passengers and surviving crew members decided to revolt against the hijackers to retake the plane. The passengers attacked the hijackers. The hijackers, realizing that they were going to be overtaken by the passengers, decided to crash the plane. The plan was to crash the plane into the White House, but the passenger revolt onboard prevented the hijackers from reaching their destination.

Khalid Sheikh Mohammed was the mastermind behind the September 11 attack. He was the one who presented the plans to attack the World Trade Center by flying planes into them. He had previously been involved in the bombing of the World Trade Center in 1993. Sometime in 1991 or 1992, Khalid Sheikh Mohammed learned of Ramzi Yousef's plan to launch an attack inside of the United States. Khalid Sheikh Mohammed discussed the progress of these plans with Yousef through numerous telephone conversations. Khalid Sheikh Mohammed also contributed funds to this plan. The 1993 bombing of the World Trade Center motivated Khalid Sheikh Mohammed to become more involved in planning attacks against the United States. Khalid Sheikh Mohammed explained that his animus towards the United States stemmed from America's support for Israel.

Following the 9/11 attack, the United States demanded that the Taliban turn over bin Laden and other Al Qaeda operatives. In his speech before a joint session of Congress, President George W. Bush declared: "Every nation, in every region, now has a decision to make: Either you are with us, or you are with the terrorists." He also explained that this war went beyond bin Laden, explaining that the war "will not end until every terrorist group of global reach has been found, stopped, and defeated."

The United States launched a military invasion of Afghanistan which forced the Taliban from power, although the Taliban would later regain power again in 2021. Bin Laden escaped being captured during the initial American invasion of Afghanistan. It was not until 2011 that the United States was finally able to locate and assassinate bin Laden.

Bin Laden did not succeed in driving America out of the region, but the ideas which bin Laden preached continued to spread beyond Al Qaeda. Al Qaeda's ideas influenced an Islamic organization in Nigeria known as Boko Haram. Boko Haram translates to Western education is forbidden. This negative attitude towards Western education stems from the fact that Western education is available to a small elite who are typically trained in British universities and then return to rule Nigeria from the capital. Yusuf Muhammad was the founder of Boko Haram. His goal was to end the rule of this elite.

Boko Haram appealed to the frustrations of northern Nigerians who struggle with poverty and lack of opportunity, as well as abuses from the government's security forces. Initially Boko Haram did not target civilian populations. Boko Haram's violent attacks were aimed at the government. The group moved in a more radical direction in 2009 after about 70 Boko Haram members attacked a mosque and police station, killing 55 people. Nigerian security forces retaliated in a crackdown which killed more than 700 people, many of whom were innocent bystanders. Yusuf was captured and paraded before television cameras before he was executed in front of a crowd outside of a police station. This action only further radicalized Boko Haram.

Weeks after the execution of Yusuf, Al Qaeda reached out to Boko Haram to express support for the organization. Boko Haram's remaining members scattered to other countries. Some of them received training in Algerian camps from Al Qaeda. Members of Boko Haram also trained in Somalia with Al Shabab, which is an Islamic organization in Somalia that is also affiliated with Al Qaeda. In 1993, Al Qaeda had sent weapons and trainers to Somalis who were fighting American forces. Bin Laden explained in an interview that he and his followers were preparing for a long struggle in Somalia, but the United States "rushed out of Somalia in shame and disgrace." The withdrawal of the American army in Somalia emboldened bin Laden.

Boko Haram returned to Nigeria as a more sophisticated and better equipped organization. Under the leadership of Abubakar Shekau, Boko Haram also began staging more lethal attacks. These attacks targeted civilians. This was done to demonstrate the incapacity of the Nigerian state. The brutality of Boko Haram has been such that even fellow jihadists have accused Boko Haram of killing too many noncombatants (The New York Times reported on this on May 7, 2014, with a story titled "Abduction of Girls an Act Not Even Al Qaeda Can Condone"). Some jihadists were shocked to hear news that Boko Haram had kidnapped schoolgirls in 2014. Bronwyn Bruton explained that the violence that African rebel groups practice "makes Al Qaeda look like a bunch of schoolgirls."

As stated before, Boko Haram did appeal to

legitimate frustrations felt by Nigerians in the north, but since 2009 the organization has become increasingly radicalized to the point that Al Qaeda has found it difficult to support some of Boko Haram's actions. By 2014, when Boko Haram kidnapped over 200 schoolgirls, Al Qaeda was moving towards a more moderate position of avoiding killing civilians for fear of losing potential supporters. Boko Haram, on the other hand, had no such fear. As Al Qaeda was moving in a more moderate direction, Boko Haram was doing the opposite.

I mention Boko Haram not only as an example of how bin Laden's brand of Islamic extremism has expanded to other parts of the world, but also to demonstrate that an insidious aspect of this brand of Islamic extremism is that it appeals to legitimate frustrations on the part of Muslims who are recruited by these organizations to carry out these heinous actions. The 9/11 Commission Report noted that the image of the United States among Muslim populations around the world was a very negative one. The 9/11 Commission Report noted that only 15% of Muslims in Indonesia held a favorable view of America, which was a sharp decline from the previous 61%. Among Muslims in Nigeria, America's favorability was 38%. The report noted that many of "these views are at best uninformed about the United States and, at worst, informed by cartoonish stereotypes, the coarse expression of a fashionable 'Occidentalism' among intellectuals who caricature U.S. values and policies." This is true, but I cannot help but feel that the report was also downplaying some of the legitimate criticisms that Muslims have of the United States, such as the continued America intervention in the political affairs of Muslim nations. This would include actions such as the military intervention in Somalia which led to the deaths of several Somalis or organizing a coup in Iran—it was noted before that bin Laden was supporting Somalis in their struggle against the United States. These interventions cannot be so easily explained away as being the result of Muslim intellectuals attempting to caricature the United States.

Bin Laden's terrorism also raised questions about the religion of Islam itself. Following the 9/11 attack, President Bush declared that "the face of terror is not the true face of Islam." Given the rapid expansion of violent Islamic terrorist groups, not everyone has been convinced. The fact is that Islam is a religion which very explicitly allows for violence within certain contexts. Whereas Jesus was an individual who rejected violence and urged his followers to turn the other cheek when struck, Muhammad was a very successful military commander. As was already noted, after Muhammad's death, the religion of Islam expanded throughout the region due to military conquests, so the spread of Islam and Arab culture has been directly connected to Arab imperialism.

I bring Africa up once again in this context because Africans were victims of Arab imperialism. The religion of Islam spread throughout North and East Africa through violent conquests. The Arab expansion also brought with it an expansive slave trade which would predate the European slave trade. During this period, some Arabs also developed some very negative racial attitudes towards Africans.

One historian explained that one of the elements of strength in Islam "lay in the insistence of Islam upon the perfect brotherhood and equality before God of all believers, whatever their colour, origin or status." Malcolm X felt compelled to drop Elijah Muhammad's interpretation of Islam and embrace orthodox Islam following his hajji to Mecca. He explained in his autobiography: "America needs to understand Islam, because this is the one religion that erases from its society the race problem." Malcolm was moved by his experience in Mecca, where he met, talked to, and ate with white people who truly saw him as a brother. This was a display of brotherhood which Malcolm had not experienced among white people in the United States.

One of the appeals of Islam is the idea that Muslims of all races are brothers and sisters who are united together in worship of a common creator. Racial unity has not always been practiced in the Arab world, however. This is demonstrated by an incident in which hundreds of Nigerian women who had made the hajj to Mecca were detained because they did not have a male escort. Some of the women complained that they were being treated like criminals for attempting to make the hajj without being accompanied by a husband or male relative. One of the women who were detained complained that more than 2,000 women were detained in an area where there was only one toilet. The women were made to go several days without bathing as well. Malcolm's experience in Mecca was a very moving one for him, but the reality is that not every African who has made the hajj to Mecca has been fortunate enough to have the experience that Malcolm had.

History demonstrates that the pacifism which Jesus preached has never stopped Christians from engaging in extreme acts of violence, but violence was not something which Jesus had expressly encouraged. The Qur'an, however, does expressly allow for defensive wars. Quran 2:191 states: "Kill them whenever you confront them and drive them out from where they drove you out. (For though killing is sinful) wrongful persecution is even worse than killing." This passage acknowledges that killing is wrong, but that wrongful persecution is even worse and for that reason killing is acceptable if the killing is done to protect oneself from wrongful persecution. Killing is treated as a serious offense in the Qur'an. It is so serious that Qur'an 5:32 declares that to kill one person would be to kill all of mankind and that to save a life would be as if to save all of mankind.

The Qur'an does allow for war, but there are also limitations on what actions can be carried out during war as well. Qur'an 2:190 cautions those who are fighting in the way of righteousness against transgression. Transgression in this verse is not specifically defined, but the intention of this verse clearly suggests that there are certain limitations in war which should be observed by righteous Muslims. A moderate Muslim would likely argue that indiscriminately killing civilians would be an act of transgression, but bin Laden was no moderate. He was a fundamentalist and a violent extremist. The legacy of bin Laden is that he promoted the spread of an Islamic ideology which advocated for extreme displays of violence targeted at civilian populations.

5 THE MURDER OF PATRICE LUMUMBA

On June 30, 1960, the Democratic Republic of Congo gained its independence. For the occasion King Baudouin delivered a speech praising Belgium's rule of the Congo and the contributions of his uncle, Leopold II. The reality was that the Congo was brutally exploited by Belgium and the Congolese people were tortured and massacred. Perhaps most insulting of all was Baudouin's claim that the Congo now had to earn the confidence of the Belgians. The Congo's president, Joseph Kasa-Vubu, spoke afterwards. Although he was angered by the speech that Baudouin made, Kasa-Vubu stuck to his prepared speech. Prime Minister Patrice Lumumba, however, could not let this pass. Lumumba was not scheduled to speak, which made what he had to say even more shocking to the Belgians.

Lumumba spoke about the injustices that the Belgians had inflicted on the Congolese and reminded the Congolese people that independence was something that they had fought to achieve. He said to the audience, "who can forget the volleys of gunfire in which so many of our brothers perished, the cells where the authorities threw those who would not submit to a rule where justice meant oppression and exploitation." The Congolese people applauded the speech, but the Belgians were not pleased by what Lumumba had to say. The Belgians were so outraged that Baudouin and his ministers considered boycotting the lunch that followed the independence ceremony. This speech would set the tone for Lumumba's strained relationship with the West.

Leading up to the Congo's independence there was growing dissatisfaction with Belgian rule. This was part of the larger movement towards independence that was sweeping across Africa. A contributing factor to the unrest in the Congo was that of the *évolué* class. These were Africans that were educated within the colonial system. The Belgians, like many Europeans, believed that creating a class of educated African elites would benefit the colonizers in controlling their colony. What the Belgians failed to foresee is that it was from these same *évolué* that the demand for independence would eventually come. Patrice Lumumba himself had come out of this class of Belgian trained elites.

The *Mouvement National Congolais* (MNC) was formed in 1958 by Lumumba and others. Lumumba's political views were largely influenced by his trip to Ghana in 1958 to attend the All-African People's Conference. Kwame Nkrumah's Convention People's Party would provide a model for Lumumba, who was determined to achieve independence for his homeland. Despite his demands for independence, Lumumba was also pro-Western in his outlook. As mentioned before, Lumumba came from the class of Africans known as *évolué*. Even after achieving independence, Lumumba continued to encourage Western investment and aid to develop the Congo. Lumumba did not envision independence to mean that the Congo would cut all ties with Belgium and wished to cooperate with Belgium as partners. Lumumba was unwilling to forget the brutalities of Belgian colonial rule in the Congo, yet he denied the charges that he was anti-white. Lumumba in fact expressed a great willingness to work with the Belgium government. He declared: "Mistakes have been made in Africa in the past, but we are ready to work with the powers which have been in Africa to create a powerful new bloc. If this does not happen, it will be the fault of the West. We are friendly to the West which has helped us up to now." Much of these views were inspired by Nkrumah, whose praise for the British had impressed Lumumba.

Lumumba was arrested in 1956 on the charge of embezzling 126,000 francs from the post office where he worked. Lumumba was sentenced to two-years, but ended up serving 12 months. This incident came to represent to some of the American officials the type of irresponsible man that they believed Lumumba to be. Allen Dulles, in particular, stated that Lumumba "was irresponsible, had been charged with embezzlement, was now being offered bribes from various sources and was supported by Belgian Communists." Lumumba was arrested again for inciting violence in 1959 when a riot broke out and a number of Africans were killed following a speech that he had given. He was released from prison to attend the Round Table Conference in Brussels. During his time in prison Lumumba was mistreated by the police, which was demonstrated by the fresh scars that he had on his wrists when he arrived at the conference.

The Round Table Conference began on January 20, 1960. Six months after the conference the Congo was to become independent. The rapid shift to independence was something that Belgium was unprepared for. The Belgians wanted a gradual transference of power, but the Congolese politicians wanted independence as quickly as possible. Belgium agreed to this and June 30 was the date set for independence. In the elections leading up to independence the MNC took the largest total with 33 seats, but the majority of those votes came from the Stanleyville province. There was little support for the MNC in Katanga and Leopoldville, which demonstrated that the MNC did not enjoy complete support throughout the nation. Although the MNC had the most seats, they held only 33 seats out of 137. Moreover, the soon-to-be independent Congolese government was made up of a shaky coalition of rivaling politicians. Kasa-Vubu was the president of this new nation and Lumumba would be the prime minister, despite the fact that both men had differing views on the question of the Congo being a unitary state. Lumumba was a Congolese nationalist, whereas Kasa-Vubu, who belonged to a political party known as the Bakongos' Alliance (Abako), wanted to achieve independence to revive the Bakongo state.

What set Lumumba apart from other Congolese politicians was that Lumumba envisioned a unified nation while other politicians remained loyal to their tribal or regional associations. It should be remembered that the Belgian Congo encompassed a wide range of different ethnic groups that were all forced to live in the same nation by the Belgians. As was the case with most African colonies, these forced borders eventually led to numerous conflicts. Lumumba's commitment to a unitary state conflicted with other Congolese politicians that believed in a federalist state and these conflicting views would later be among the many things that divided Congolese politicians following independence. Looking at the problems in the post-colonial Congo, one cannot help but think that a federalist state could have alleviated some of that. Colin Legum explained: "Lumumba's great political error is that he tried to cast the Congo into the tight mould of Ghana, rather than into the larger, more accommodating mould of Nigeria."

There was much hope and optimism about the Congo's independence. This optimism was perhaps best captured by Le Grand Kallé in the song "Indépendance Cha Cha." This hope quickly evaporated as the Congo was thrown into crisis shortly after achieving independence. In "Indépendance Cha Cha," Le Grand Kallé celebrated the fact that leading political parties and politicians of the Congo were able to come together and unite at the Round Table conference. He sings:

ASORECO and ABAKO

United as one

CONAKAT and CARTEL

Had joined the Front Commun

Bolikango, Kasavubu,

Lumumba and Kalonji

Bolya, Tshombe, Kamitatu,

Oh Essandja, and Elder Kanza[1]

The first serious problem facing the Congo was an army mutiny, which broke out only a few days after independence. The Congolese soldiers were already increasingly frustrated due to the low pay and lack of promotion that they had to endure. They became disillusioned with the reality that despite the Congo having gained its independence, conditions did not change for them. Though the government was under Congolese control, Belgians still controlled the army. To make this point clear an officer named Emile Janssens wrote on a blackboard declaring "Before independence=after independence." This led to a protest in which soldiers demanded that Janssens be dismissed. Lumumba blamed this rebellion on the Belgians and he dismissed Janssens and replaced the officer corps with Congolese. Among those that were promoted was Joseph Mobutu, who was a personal aide for Lumumba. This did little to quell the mutiny, however.

In response to this, the Belgian government landed troops in the Congo against the wishes of Lumumba. The Belgian troops took control of key locations in the Congo. Lumumba began to see this as a plot by Belgium to undermine the Congo's independence. Complicating matters was that the Katanga region in the Congo seceded under the leadership of Moise Tshombe, who declared Katanga to be an independent

---

[1] Lyrics translated here from the original Lingala version.

state. Belgium supported and provided assistance to Tshombe, which further strained the relationship between Lumumba and the Belgian government. The Belgians also supported another secessionist movement in South Kasai, which was led by Albert Kalonji. Kalonji was a member of the MNC and Lumumba's chief lieutenant, but differences between the two led Kalonji to form a breakaway faction of the MNC.

Desperately looking for assistance, Lumumba turned to the United Nations for assistance, but Lumumba's relationship with the UN proved to be a difficult one. In the first place, Lumumba had expected that the UN would forcibly remove the Belgian army, but he was upset to find that he could not use the UN forces as his own personal army to quell the secession. Brian Urquhart explained that Lumumba wanted a military solution to the secession whereas the UN's mandate had prevented them from getting involved in a military conflict. The UN also wanted to work towards a peaceful solution, which Lumumba apparently did not have the patience for.

Dag Hammarskjöld was the UN official who was tasked with resolving the crisis in the Congo. Hammarskjöld found himself in a difficult position and his dealings with Lumumba were frustrating. In one instance, Hammarskjöld decided not to take Lumumba with him on a trip to Katanga to work towards the withdrawal of the Belgian troops. Hammarskjöld believed that Lumumba's presence would have complicated the mission, but Lumumba was outraged by this and attacked Hammarskjöld. Lumumba had similar disputes with other UN officials. Ralph Bunche, an African American, was the head of the UN operation in the Congo. The relationship between the two became so strained that Lumumba eventually refused to work with Bunche. Bunche reported that "Lumumba was crazy and that he reacted like a child." Lumumba was apparently not fond of Bunche either. Lumumba angrily demanded to know why Hammarskjöld sent *"ce negre Americain"* to the Congo.

With the Belgian troops out of the Congo, Lumumba now wanted the UN troops to be used to quell the secession of Katanga. He insisted that UN forces "be used to subdue the rebel government in Katanga." The UN's mandate prevented this, however. They could not quell the secession in Katanga by force and instead they planned to work towards a peaceful settlement of the issue. Lumumba was unsatisfied by this and once again lashed out at UN officials, accusing them of collaborating with Belgium. Urquhart explains that Lumumba's dealings with the UN "deteriorated into a bewildering series of pleas for assistance, threats, and ultimatums." Urquhart further notes that Lumumba "issued impossible demands and expected instant results." Urquhart ultimately concluded that he could not pretend that trying to help Lumumba "was a pleasant or rewarding experience."

Frustrated with the lack of resolution that the UN brought to the situation in the Congo, Lumumba decided to go on a trip to Washington in July to gain American support. This was a difficult task given that America had already considered Lumumba to be a communist sympathizer and had little desire to work with Lumumba. Lumumba's trip to Washington did little to win him American support, but it seemed to confirm to American officials that Lumumba was not someone that they could trust. American under-secretary of state, Douglas Dillon, described Lumumba as being "an irrational, almost 'psychotic' personality." Dillon concluded that Lumumba was "impossible to deal with." Thomas Cassilly described Lumumba as being "impulsive," "unstable," and prone to making rash decisions. One example of this was when Lumumba granted a multimillion dollar financial concession to L. Edgar Detwiler, against the advice of some of his advisors and members of his cabinet. These plans never went through, but for Cassilly this exemplified Lumumba's tendency to make rash and ill-advised decisions. According to Cassilly, during his trip to Washington, Lumumba had also requested that he have a female companion to spend the night with. When asked what type of woman he had in mind, Lumumba responded "*Une blanche blonde*." The CIA arranged a meeting for Lumumba in a nearby hotel and Lumumba expressed his satisfaction the next morning. Cassilly concluded that the Soviet Union would have found Lumumba just as difficult to deal with as he and other American diplomats did.

The comments made by both UN and US officials attest to Lumumba's often erratic behavior. Lumumba's erratic behavior also made it difficult for African states to support him, as Legum explains:

> Although the African States were willing to give full backing to Lumumba's Government, the Prime Minister's erratic policies imposed an increasing strain on their loyalty as August lengthened into September. It was not only that he was difficult to deal with; his personal quarrels with Dr Ralph Bunche and Mr

Hammarskjöld, his nagging doubts about the UN and especially his connivance at attacks on UN personnel by members of the Force Publique, and his private negotiations with the Russians, all contributed to dissension and division.

The lack of support that Lumumba had from African states is demonstrated by the "Little Summit" of African states that was held in Leopoldville from August 25 to 31. By the end of the summit, only the Guineans agreed with Lumumba's critical position on the UN. The others praised the work of the UN and sent a message of appreciation to Dr. Ralph Bunche. These African states also opposed the secession movements, but offered little in terms of actually helping to put down Tshombe's secession.

The previously mentioned comments by Cassilly and Dillon must also be understood in the context of America's attempts at undermining Lumumba. American depictions of Lumumba described him as being an incompetent, authoritarian, corrupt, and unstable leader to justify their own opposition to his politics. Jonathan J. Cole explains: "Lacking any concrete evidence of corruption or malfeasance on the part of the democratically elected Prime Minister, U.S. officials resorted to personal attacks as a means of discrediting Lumumba's authority and justifying his removal." American officials often exaggerated Lumumba's faults, particularly concerning the danger he posed. Frank Carlucci, an officer in the American embassy in Leopoldville who knew Lumumba personally, explained:

He was not as dangerous as portrayed. I didn't think he was a Communist. He was passionate, mercurial, and initially correct regarding the need for a unified Congo. I didn't like his means, cozying up to the Soviets, his erraticism, but didn't view him as an overwhelming threat.

One of the many accusations hurled at Lumumba was that he was a communist who was a puppet of the Soviet Union. Lumumba himself denied that he was a communist. Lumumba made his views clear when he explained:

> We are simply Africans. We do not want to subject ourselves to any foreign influence, we want nothing to do with any imported doctrines, whether from the West, from Russia, or from America. The Congo remains the Congo. We are Africans. We want to make the Congo a great free nation. We do not want to escape one dictatorship only to fall beneath another.

Although Lumumba denied that he was a communist, he became a target for America when he requested help from the Soviet Union to deal with the situation in Katanga. The involvement of the Soviet Union and the United States in the Congo complicated the Congo's problems even further by turning the nation into yet another battleground for the Cold War. Lumumba's threats to enlist Soviet help if the UN did not give into his demands also displeased some of the African leaders that had supported Lumumba.

The Eisenhower administration decided that

Lumumba had to be eliminated and they began plotting ways to get rid of the prime minister. This included a plot to poison Lumumba's toothpaste. Another one of the plots to eliminate Lumumba was a plan to smuggle Lumumba out of his UN guarded residence. The plot was to be carried through by a European, known as "QJWIN," who was to pretend to be UN officer in order to enter Lumumba's residence and escort him out, but this plot was ruined when Lumumba secretly escaped from his house the next day. The Belgians were also plotting Lumumba's assassination as well, but none of their schemes ever took off.

Lumumba's erratic actions alienated many Congolese politicians. Nothing represents this better than Lumumba's decision to send a military expedition to South Kasai. This expedition resulted in the deaths of hundreds of Baluba and thousands more becoming refugees. The events in South Kasai reflected badly on Lumumba's government. Hammarskjöld described the event as having "the characteristics of the crime of genocide." Cassilly describes it as a "disastrous" attack that "embarrassed" Lumumba's "Soviet backers." The expedition in South Kasai also increased Kalonji's distrust and hatred of Lumumba. Kalonji described Lumumba as an "assassin" and called for his execution. In February 1961, a number of Lumumba's supporters were transferred to South Kasai where they were gruesomely executed. In response to the attack on South Kasai, Kasa-Vubu accused Lumumba of poor governance and plunging the Congo into chaos. He dismissed Lumumba as prime minister and appointed Joseph Ileo instead. Lumumba in turn took to the radio to announce that he had dismissed Kasa-Vubu as president. The Parliament reacted by annulling both announcements, but the actions of both men divided the nation and fueled Cold War tensions in the Congo. Kasa-Vubu was backed by America and Lumumba was backed by the Soviet Union.

In order to prevent the situation from becoming more divisive, the UN organization in the Congo, without the consent of Hammarskjöld, decided to close the Leopoldville radio. When Lumumba attempted to force his way into the radio station he was barred by Ghanaian troops that were acting under the orders of the UN. Kwame Nkrumah, who had been in correspondence with Lumumba throughout the whole ordeal, wrote to Lumumba to explain that the Ghanaian troops were acting on the orders of the UN and urged Lumumba to continue working with the UN. He also urged Lumumba to work with Kasa-Vubu. Nkrumah wrote: "You cannot afford, my brother, to be harsh and uncompromising. Do not force Kasavubu out now. It will bring you too much trouble in Leopoldville when you want calm there now." Although Lumumba did not heed Nkrumah's advice, Nkrumah was right. The dispute between Lumumba and Kasa-Vubu brought trouble to Leopoldville.

The situation became even more complicated when Mobutu, with the support of the United States, neutralized the civilian government in Leopoldville. Mobutu created a new interim government in which Kasa-Vubu served as president, but Lumumba and all of his supporters were excluded from this new government. Moreover, Mobutu had issued an arrest warrant for Lumumba, who was still living at the prime minister's residence in Leopoldville. Hammarskjöld refused to recognize Mobutu's new government and instead worked towards reconciling Lumumba and

Kasa-Vubu in order to restore the civilian government. At this point the Congo was in dire need of a stable government to address issues such as the empty treasury. The United States was not pleased by Hammarskjöld's position on the issue and even threatened to withdraw their support from the UN's operation in the Congo.

Lumumba was guarded by the UN troops to protect him from being arrested by Mobutu's troops. The UN was fiercely criticized by America for protecting Lumumba. Throughout the whole ordeal, the UN was being denounced by all sides. America, Belgium, the Soviets, Lumumba, and Mobutu were all displeased by the UN's actions for one reason or another. In the end, America was successful in getting the UN to recognize the new government. In the meantime, Lumumba was isolated at his UN protected residence.

The UN had warned Lumumba that to leave his residence would be putting himself at risk, but this was a risk that Lumumba was willing to take. Lumumba managed to sneak out of his residence, hidden in a car. Lumumba then set about trying to reach his supporters in Stanleyville, but during the journey he stopped in a number of villages along the way to give speeches. This made it easier for Lumumba's enemies to catch up with him and they eventually arrested him. Lumumba was tied up and brought to the airport at Leopoldville. He was publicly beaten and humiliated in front of news reporters. Throughout the entire ordeal Lumumba refused to beg for mercy or to change his defiant demeanor. This would be the last time that Lumumba would ever be seen publicly.

Despite the West's apprehension towards Lumumba, Lumumba constantly attempted to reaffirm his willingness to work with the West to develop the Congo. At the Round Table Conference in Belgium, Lumumba had explained: "We know the Congolese are not sufficiently prepared to experience sovereignty. The Belgians know it too. But I am delighted with the Belgian spirit. Now white and black can help each other to build up the country, with each playing his proper role." Lumumba's attempt to force a deal with Detwiler, against the desires of his cabinet, certainly demonstrates Lumumba's willingness to work with Western financers. Neither Belgium nor the United States were ever completely trusting of Lumumba, however.

With Lumumba eliminated, the United States needed someone to replace Lumumba. Cassilly explains that "in the end, the United States invested billions in Joseph Mobutu, who did accomplish what Washington wanted: keeping the USSR out of the Congo for the remaining years of the Cold War." One CIA agent named O'Donnell had referred to Mobutu as "our close instrument, he was the man we had put our chips on." Devlin also affirmed that he had been working closely with Mobutu as an advisor.

Mobutu renamed the Congo to Zaire. Zaire was like Mobutu's personal property, mirroring the way Leopold II had controlled the Congo. Mobutu made a fortune from exploiting his people while also enjoying close relations with the Western world, especially with the United States and France. American military aid assisted Mobutu to stay in power in the face of numerous attempts to overthrow him. American President Ronald Reagan described Mobutu as "a voice of good sense and good will." Reagan's successor, George H.W. Bush, described Mobutu as "one of our most valued friends." Bush added, "I was honored to invite President Mobutu to be the first African head of state to come to the United States for an official visit during my presidency."

This honored guest of the White House plundered his nation's treasury to the point that by 1993 there was no money to pay the army and state officials. Soldiers responded to this by rioting. They looted shops, homes, and government buildings, killing hundreds in the process. Corruption and theft reached a point where the American embassy advised its staff not to unlock their car doors or roll down their windows when stopped by the police at roadblocks. They recommended simply showing their papers through the windows of their car to avoid being robbed. By the time that Mobutu was overthrown he was one of the richest men in the world, having an estimated $4 billion. He owned a yacht, a private jet, and homes in various European countries.

Mobutu was finally driven out of the Congo during the First Congo War, in which Rwanda led an invasion in Zaire. At the time of the war Mobutu had few allies in Africa and the West. As a result of the war Mobutu was ousted and Laurent-Désiré Kabila became the president. On May 17, 1997, Kabila swore in as the president of the newly renamed Democratic Republic of Congo. Kabila was praised as being a "new breed" of African leader. Yoweri Museveni of Uganda claimed that Kabila had "liberated not only the Congo but all of Africa." Kabila played into this by portraying himself as Lumumba's true successor. The problem was that Kabila differed very little with Mobutu. Kabila banned political parties. He also gave political positions to his close friends and family members. Those who were accused of engaging in political activities were detained. This included journalists. Kabila was eventually assassinated in 2001.

Of course, it is difficult to say whether or not Lumumba could have succeeded in developing his nation, where so many other African politicians had failed. Lumumba was certainly committed to his nation's independence, a cause he was willing to die for. Moreover, unlike other politicians Lumumba wanted a united Congo that was free of tribalism and other divisions. Yet, as has been noted, he was often known to make questionable and rash decisions, which no doubt contributed to the prevailing chaos in the Congo. Martin Meredith concludes that Lumumba "possessed no plan of action or strategy and his habit of taking impulsive and arbitrary decisions quickly alienated many of his Congolese allies." Much of Lumumba's missteps can be attributed to his own inexperience as a political leader. Legum explains that "Lumumba's mistakes were due partly to his mercurial personality, partly to his one fixed idea - belief in the unitary state – and partly to his inexperience." Prior to becoming the prime minister, Lumumba worked in a post office and as the director of a brewery, but neither job prepared him to run a nation, especially one as complex as the Congo.

Following his death Lumumba became a heroic symbol of African independence and a martyr for the Congo. For all the missteps that Lumumba made in handling the crisis in the Congo, he was a man who was committed to the liberation and development of his nation. In the aftermath of his assassination, the Congo has been one of the most impoverished, unstable, and war torn nations in Africa. Lumumba's vision was the complete independence of the Congo and for a while he had achieved this goal, but like so many African nations the Congo's independence was undermined by a combination of personal greed and incompetence on the part of African politicians, as well as Western imperialist interests.

References:

Adam Hochschild, *King Leopold's Ghost*, (New York: Mariner Books, 1998).

Brian Urquhart, "The Tragedy of Lumumba," *The New York Reviewer*, October 4, 2001.

Colin Legum, *Congo Disaster*, (Penguin Books Inc., 1961).

Jonathan J. Cole, "The Congo question: Conflicting visions of independence," *Emporia State Research Studies*, Vol. 43, no. 1, p. 26-37, 2006.

Martin Meredith, *The Fate of Africa*

Stephen R. Weissman, "An Extraordinary Rendition," *Intelligence and National Security*, 25:2, 198-222, 2010.

Thomas A. Cassilly, "A Review of: 'The Lumumba Conundrum," *International Journal of Intelligence and CounterIntelligence*, 21:1, 150-153, 2007.

www.ingramcontent.com/pod-product-compliance
Lightning Source LLC
Chambersburg PA
CBHW051702250726
48653CB00007B/2794